# Arthur Lost His Mojo

## By

## Alison Stephens

eBook ISBN: 978-1-965161-51-7

Paperback ISBN: 978-1-965161-52-4

# Dedication

I lovingly dedicate this book to my cherished children, Paul, Gary, and Kelly, and to my wonderful grandsons, Conor, Garin, Jacob, Bailey, and Jared.

A special mention goes to my great-grandson, Brady, who represents the joy of future generations.

May this work inspire and protect the world they will inherit.

# About The Author

Alison Stephens was born and brought up in a small town of Abergavenny, South Wales, United Kingdom. As the years went by, she got married and had three wonderful children.

Over time, nothing significant happened until she came across Sandra Rushton of Santangle (a posh form of doodling) and, in particular, a stencil set called Locket Lane.

This discovery triggered her writing journey, leading to the creation of Arthur the Elf Shelf and many other works that will be published in the future.

*Illustrated*
*by*
*Kayleigh Bundy*

# Arthur Lost His Mojo

After twenty-four days of Christmas skullduggery and mischief, Arthur was exhausted and ready to put his feet up, so once his last trick was done, he headed back to his cottage where he could have a nice cup of tea and relax.

He slumped into his favorite armchair, letting out a heavy sigh as he looked at the mess of prank materials scattered around the room. Empty boxes, colorful streamers, and glitter from his last escapade lay in disarray. "Ah, what a season," he mumbled to himself, his eyes growing heavy.

For the next month or so, Arthur did nothing but sleep and lounge around his cottage.

But soon, even lounging became boring. Arthur found himself staring at the ceiling for hours on end, wondering what to do. "I need a spark, something new... but where to find it?" He fiddled with an old prank gadget on his desk, but the joy of mischief didn't come to him as it once did.

Arthur then realized that he needed to start preparing for the coming year's skullduggery and mischief, so for the next couple of months, he was trying to come up with new ideas and tricks he could do, but nothing was coming to mind.

"I've lost it," he said, tossing crumpled paper ideas into the waste bin.

It seemed that he had a trickery block, Arthur was becoming worried that he wouldn't be able to make children (not so much the parents) happy this year.

Arthur thought about faking his own kidnapping and started to make plans on how he could put it into action, Arthur was going to say that unless the owls and the children's families came up with ideas for mischief, they would not see him again.

He began writing ransom notes to send out to the owls and families but then thought because he was known as the naughty elf, "Maybe the owls and families would think it was just one of Arthur's pranks and ignore the notes. Maybe they would be happy I was kidnapped," he muttered to himself. So, he decided this wasn't such a good idea after all and ditched the kidnapping plan.

"No, that won't do," Arthur said, scrapping the note. "I need something truly clever— something they've never seen before." His mind wandered to his most famous pranks of past years, trying to find a new twist on old classics. "Maybe... no, too boring," he mumbled, crumpling another paper.

One morning, Obie Owl (who was one of the wisest owls in the world) dropped by for a cup of tea and cake. Obie could see that Arthur was looking sad and asked , "What's the matter, Arthur?"

Arthur replied, "I have been a lazy elf this year and have left everything to the last minute. I am feeling stressed as I cannot think of any new ideas to cause mischief this year, and then children will start to forget about me and find something else to do over the Christmas month. Oh, what am I going to do? I don't want the children to forget me. I love causing mischief, and I know the children love it too!!"

Obie reminded Arthur that he should have been preparing for this months ago and not be lazing about; Arthur knew this was true because he already thought that.

"But what if I've lost my touch for good?" Arthur said, pacing around the room. Obie watched him, tapping his beak thoughtfully.

Obie said he would get together with other wise owls around the world and see if they would be willing to help. I am not promising they will help, but I can only ask. Arthur was overjoyed and very grateful that Obie was going to help him.

Over the coming days and weeks, Arthur was inundated with notelets from different owls with ideas and suggestions on how he could cause mischief. He was humbled by the response and kindness he had received from the Owls and others who were willing to help him out.

One day, a particularly large package arrived at his door. When Arthur opened it, he found a strange assortment of items: a rainbow-colored balloon, a jar of glitter, and a note that read,

"For your grandest prank yet—combine with care!" Arthur chuckled, already imagining the chaos he could create.

Arthur began looking through the ideas and suggestions he had received and began sorting through them all from good to not-so-good, but, they would all work if he tweaked them a little.

There were two suggestions that caught Arthur's eye. One was to make a sponge cake with a note saying, "Out of the kindness of my heart, I have made you a delicious cake!"

The other was to put the child's favorite toy in a bucket tied up and suspended from balloons with a note saying, "I'm a celebrity; get me out of here."

Arthur grinned, his energy renewed as he worked late into the night. "This year is going to be the best one yet," he whispered as he hung the balloons and prepared his sponge cake prank.

The other one was to put the child's favourite toy in a bucket, tied up and suspended from the balloons with a note saying, "I'm a celebrity; get me out of here."

As the Christmas month was only around the corner Arthur knew that he now had plenty of ideas to cause mischief to families around the world.

He even added a few new tricks that he hadn't tried before—one involving disappearing gifts and another involving a mysterious snowball fight invitation that never actually happened!

Arthur's Christmas month went well and homes all over the world were full of joy and laughter to the mischief he had caused.

As the Christmas season drew to a close, Arthur slumped back into his armchair, exhausted but satisfied. He looked around his cozy cottage, which was now filled with the remnants of pranks and the joyful clutter of a season well-spent. Smiling to himself, he whispered, "I've still got it."

Just then, a familiar tap came at his window. Obie Owl was perched outside, a knowing gleam in his eye. Arthur opened the window, and Obie hooted, "Well done, Arthur. You've made this season unforgettable."

Arthur chuckled. "Thanks to you and all the wise owls. I couldn't have done it alone."

With a final wink, Obie flew off into the night, leaving Arthur to bask in the quiet satisfaction of a job well done. As he drifted off to sleep, Arthur knew one thing for certain: he would always find his way back to the mischief and magic that made him, well, Arthur the Naughty Elf.

And as for the children? They would surely wake up on Christmas morning with wide-eyed wonder, already excited for next year's pranks, not knowing what delightful chaos Arthur might dream up next.

Arthur grinned in his sleep, his heart full of joy and his spirit ready for whatever mischief lay ahead.

*Inspired By Sandra Rushton*

*Sanntangle*

www.ingramcontent.com/pod-product-compliance
Lightning Source LLC
Chambersburg PA
CBHW051254120626
46547CB00014B/1937